D1560719

Darling covered his house ★ inside and out—even the chairs ★ roof ★ doors ★ and refrigerators—with hundreds of paintings ★ In Possum Trot ★ out in the desert ★ an eerie Doll Theater was put together by Calvin and Ruby Black ★ In Jacumba ★ M.T. Ratcliffe spent his spare time carving fantastic animals out of rock ★ a six-foot-high skull ★ buffalo ★ snakes ★ lizards ★ In Fresno ★ Baldessare Forestiere found that the land he had bought for a farm had hardpan instead of soil ★ So he carved out acres of walkways ★ rooms ★ gardens ★ and patios for his unfulfilled dream of a drive-in restaurant ★ fifteen feet underground ★ This is Seymour Rosen's world ★ the one he started photographing more than twenty years ago ★ Here is the key along with the combination ★ password and clue ★ If we but open our eyes to the world around us ★ we can see what Seymour Rosen has seen ★ and we will take from this collection the same lifting of the eye and spirit ★

In Celebration of Ourselves

by Seymour Rosen

Introduction by Beth Coffelt

A California Living Book

Published in Association with
the San Francisco Museum of Modern Art

First Edition

Photographs copyright © 1979 Seymour Rosen
Text copyright © 1979 California Living Books,
The San Francisco Examiner Division of The Hearst Corporation.
Special Projects, Suite 223, The Hearst Building,
Third and Market Streets, San Francisco, California 94103.

Printed in the United States of America.

ISBN 0-89395-007-6 (hardback)
ISBN 0-89395-008-4 (paperback)
Library of Congress Catalog Card Number 78-052508

Designed by David Broom
Production by David Charlsen

To Carolyn and Libby and Cheryl
and my elder brother Jerry, all of
whom I've never been able to tell I love.

To Henry Hopkins and Walter
Hopps and Don Erkel, who have
been supportive of my dreams for
more than twenty years.

And to Bernard Rudofsky,
whose books made my mind click
into understanding the patterns
of my world.

And, oops, I almost forgot —
To
William Averett
Neil Averill
Michael Aldrich
Albion Knitting Mills
Antioch College/West
Art Center School of Design
Arts Manpower Center
Advocates for the Arts
Charles Almarez
Herb Andree
Jill Anthony
Didi Atkinson
Bill and Franchesca Alpert
Roberto Albanese
AMF Corporation
Associated Press
Al and Mary Butler
Art Beal
John Beach
Ed Beral
Kermit Bishop
Calvin and Ruby Black
Harold Bagdasarian
Sarah Binder
James Brucker
Dickens 44 Bascom
Hobart Brown
Rita Bottoms
John and Bernie Blaine
Bonnie Barrett
Ralph and Anne Bennett
Jane Jordan Browne
Pascal Breunot
Howard and Susan Bilow
Mel and Joey Bilow
Susan Hooper Billstein
Roger Brown
Reba Bass
Brockman Gallery
David Beach
Ruth Baker
Dr. Richard Brown
Cherie Brown
Jan Butterfield
Judy Baca
Boy Scouts of America

Gene Brooks
Greg Blaisdale
Jules Backus
Tyrone Brue
Duke and Francis Cahill
R. G. Canning Productions
Charles Clayton
Jerry Clarke
Classics Car Club
Eileen Cusimano
Elizabeth Chaney
Edmund Carpenter
Beth Coffelt
Cliff Cheney
William Cartwright
Floyd Campbell
John Caruthers
"Crazy Painters"
Julia Cheever
Eugenie Candau
Rolando Castellon
Janice Campbell
Denise Chegaray
Cars of the Stars
Jennie Chinn
Gustavo Cardenas
Betty Carr
Senator Alan Cranston
Donald Darling
Sanford Darling
Dean Dennis
Don Deschwanden
William Dutcher
Disneyland
Tom-Barney-Carlos-Erica
  Davidson
Marcia and Joanne Dresner
Carlos and Sunday Diniz
Paul B. Dowling
Jean Duncan
Mary Lou Dresak
Tim Drescher
Peter and Lyndia D'Aprix
Kenneth and Dion Dillon
The Docents of the San Francisco
  Museum of Modern Art
John Ehn
Joanne Epstein

Rudy Esquivel
Don and Billie and Susan Erkel
James Elliot
Donald Engstrom
Fred Engleberg
Charles and Ray Eames
Herman Fayal
Rick and Lorraine Forestiere
John Fitzrandolph
Gary Fink
Dr. Kenneth Fox
Michele Ferrone
Pat Ferraro
Richard Frazier
Charles Felix
John Follis
Janice Felgar
Rosemarie Farish
Suzanne Foley
Ed Farrell
Tommy the Greek
Carolyn Dilks Gomm
Steven Goldstein
Roberto Gildemontes
Bob Gambles Photo Supply
Luckman Glasgow
Aaron Gallop
Galeria de la Raza
Gronk
Bud Goldstone
Connie Goldsmith
Dan Greenburg
Ray Girvigian
Henry Gardner
Greenburg and Glusker
Kim Harper
Nancy Hoskins
Horst
Himsl and Haas
Ed Hardy
Hatos-Hall Productions
Kay Thornton-Hirsch
Von Dutch Holland
Brian Holmes
George Herzak
Linda Ray Hulbert
Judith Hoffberg
Mikki Herman

Michael and Carolyn Harris
Joan Hugo
Michael and Sylvia Hannon
Willie Herron
Ron Herman
Kathy Holland
Bonita Hughes
Hattie Hanson
Marland and Genevieve Hoskins
Alberto L. Hurtado
Jimmy Heaslet
Industrial Photographic
  Equipment Company
Immaculate Heart College
International Show Car
  Association
International Federation
  of Van Owners
Imperials Car Club
Samuel L. Jones
John Johnson
Mel Johnson
Phil Jones
Davy Jones
Patty Jones
Michael Jones
Lyn Keinholz
Larry Kumferman
Ron and Mary Kenner
Mrs. Konya
Louise Katzman
Ted and Maty Kramer
Lucille Krasne
David Kahn
Kern County Fair
Ed Keinholz
Ron and Penelope and
  Maxwell Kullaway
Susan King
Nickolas King
Charles Kasling
Sister Karen
Kit and Susan Lukas
Megan and Gabby and
  Arthur Lukas
Phil Linhares
Harold Logsdon
Jules Lamelle

Los Angeles Fine Arts Squad
Jack Levine
Los Angeles County Fair
Jack and Mona London
Thomas W. Leavitt
Martha Lifson
Los Angeles County
    Recreation & Parks
    Cultural Affairs Department
Los Angeles City Recreation &
    Parks
Lichty Photo Murals
Al and Phyllis Lutjean
Judith Luther
Cheryl Lenz
Sally Lew
Los Angeles Times
Ted Loring
Irving and Ann Leventhal
Vicki Leon
Alle Light
Jill Lossen
Latham and Watkins
La Flor de Mexico Bakery
Los Angeles County Sheriff's
    Department
Tom Myer
Alberta Mayo
C.C. Miller
John and Frances Medica
Nolan Mahara
Miles Mahan
Bill Moeller
Joel Mark
Metal Flake Corporation
Myron Moskwa
Jack Massey
John McDougall
Kathy McManus
Jack Mays
Alex and Phyllis Madonna
Bill Morrison
Kip Mesirow
Mechicano Art Center
Ted McKinley
Daniel Martinez
Ray McQuire
Mural Resource Center

Bruce Merrifield
Michael McCone
Mujeres Muralistas
Dr. Knox Mellon
Irwin Mussen
John Merritt
Claudia Natalia
Arlen Ness
Dennis A. Newman
Ed Neiss
Maurice and Bea Nafshun
Jim Nutt
National Endowment for the Arts
National Street Rod Association
NORML
Neighborhood Arts Projects
National Hot Rod Association
Susan Olivier
William Osmun
Optic Nerve
Open Space Teachers Center
Tressa "Grandma" Prisbrey
Dudley B. Perkins
Carl Porter
Douglas Parker
Pacific Promotions
Monroe Price
Lois Pine
Suzanne, Bridget and Galen
    Palmer
Project Heavy
Allen Porter
Ray Pierce
Mel Pierce Camera
Ron and Phyllis Patterson
David Pann
Noah Purifoy
Tim-Alison-Joshua Pine
Marie Peckinpah
Al Pine
William M. Padgett
Richard Posner
Otto Roehrick
Ed Roth
Marvin Rand
Audrey Garcia Rawlings
Frank Romero
Dick Roodzant

Drs. Arnold and Barbara Rubin
David-Landra-Joshua Rosenthal
Jerry and Muriel Rosen
John Rogers
Nancy Rolf
Redding Public Library-Reference
Mary Miles Ryan
Nancy Ringler
Helen Saavedra
Self-Help Graphics
Ski and Carmen Szladowski
San Francisco
    Museum of Modern Art
Joe Shields
Sacramento Bee
Yvonne and John Selby
Rob Selway
Christine Schlesinger
Shirley Samuels
Sanger Herald
Merki Simpkins
R.L. Stallsmith
Michael Sanchez
Bill Sanders
Karen Spangenberg
Mal and Sandra Sharpe
Joe Santos
Street Freaks Car Club
Richard Stedry
Randy Smith
Mary Ann Stevenson
Sgt. Tom Skaggs
Brian Stevens
Art Seidenbaum
Barry Sanders
Leonard Schwartz
John Spencer
S.C. St. John
Studio Watts
John Sherrell
William Squyers
Irving Saraf
Jay Stewart
Tom and Barbara Taylor
Bill Tynell
Ruth Y. Tamura
Lyle Tuttle
Kent Twitchell

Rene Tabaldo
Doni Tunheim
Mel Tearle
Melody Todd
Eli-Donna-David Taub
Ida Lauren Trimmer
Alan Teel
Carolee Trefts
Kay Tolladay
Ham Tindall
Cliff Trammell
Robert B. Turnbull
Ski and Sandy Tynski
Fred Usher
John Vorhes
Ray and Dolores Vellutini
Harold and Erica Van Pelt
Estaban Villa
Mary Vangi
Ellen Van Fleet
Committee for Simon Rodia's
    Towers in Watts
Lonnie Wilson
Tom Wynne
Jeff Wachs
Bob and Elaine Weiner
Richard Wurman
Jim Woods
Jean and Kathy White
Julius Wasserstein
Robert Whyte
R.O. White
Latham and Watkins
John Williams
Rhoda Weyr
Jim Willse
Steve Young
Susan Yewell
Rene Yanez
Frank Yorba
Wako Yasunari
Mary Young
Sid Zaro
Charles-Alice-Rachael-Erica
    Zlatkoff
Bob and Jean Zuver
and thanks to all the others whose
    names somehow got left out

Acknowledgments

I wish to thank Beth Coffelt for her enthusiasm, terrible puns, wonderful meals and sensitivity to the material. Elaine Ratner and Tim Ware for their patience and skills in taking my many hours of ramblings and turning them into coherent statements. David Broom for giving life to what could have been a series of static images. Hal Silverman and Henry Hopkins for their faith in the material. Douglas Parker for his beautiful photographic prints. Nancy Hoskins for her imagination and care in doing the many hours of dirty work to pull the material together for the book. And Nancy Hoskins again for her "oh gods" when I got carried away with my own brilliance. The National Endowment for the Arts, the San Francisco Museum of Modern Art, the AMF Corporation and Studio Watts for their support. And the hundreds of artists who produced the images this book exhibits.

Preface

To a kid coming from Chicago in the early '50s California was still the "wild West." The Hollywood I thought was there didn't exist, but the frontier did—and freedom.

I took the Dodge out on Sundays and wandered the map. Here I saw the multitudes of unusual things I was never privy to in Chicago: giant donuts, a sphinx behind a store, unbelievable cars and motorcycles, castles, Roman villas, and the Watts Towers—a magical world created from what most people would consider junk. I began to photograph these wonders, and I've never stopped.

My need to document and save and share has always been impulsive. So it was up to others to tell me what I was doing. Art historians started telling me I had a great collection of contemporary folk art. A schoolteacher showed some of my slides to her kids. They loved them. She told me I had a great teaching device. Then a sociologist told me I was "building a catalog of social indicators." An anthropologist said I was becoming "an archivist of popular culture." I remember that was the day I opened my closet and said "Aha!"

For me the magic has always been in watching people getting turned on to "street art" and then producing their own. Only the most pedantic, egotistical or fearless witnesses to these phenomena have tried to fit them into particular categories. But they defy categorization, and that fact has resulted in an ongoing battle to get institutions to recognize the value of documenting and preserving these forms of expression.

Collecting the material has been, of necessity, a labor of love—for me and for others who have a similar concern. Uncredentialized things generally don't get wide acknowledgment. But I am told that perhaps the time has come; perhaps a varied and complete record of the most ephemeral events of the American spirit and heritage can finally be assembled for us all to share. Maybe we will even be able to preserve the environments and objects so that people can see them firsthand.

In Celebration of Ourselves is an attempt to move in that direction, to acknowledge the magic made available to us by those whose work looks best outside of institutional walls—with the hope that we all will take the time to do our own explorations.

Seymour Rosen
Los Angeles, 1978

Introduction

In January of 1977 Seymour Rosen was in San Francisco about to close his show "In Celebration of Ourselves — California," the finale of a series of Bicentennial exhibitions at the San Francisco Museum of Modern Art.

A schoolteacher walked through, shepherding a flock of gifted students.

"She was mad," Seymour recalls. "She was furious. She kept saying 'where's the art?' She'd come a long way to show art to her class. She couldn't find any.

"I guess it was my show that ticked her off, but she was mad about a show of rock posters, too, and a few other things. Nothing was the way she'd pictured it."

Seymour's show happened to contain hundreds of photographs that he has spent more than half his forty-two years taking, depicting the myriad forms of unheralded art available to anybody in the state of California: tattoos, costumes, hairstyles, decorated vans and trucks, painted motorcycles, fairs and pageants, neighborhood murals, storefront churches, handpainted advertising, handmade houseboats, a village made from bottles, the Watts Towers.

He views the cultural myopia evidenced by that frustrated schoolteacher with a chagrin mixed with humor, resignation, dismay, exasperation and anger.

"It was the frame she was looking for," he says. "The frame, the label, the pedestal. Take those away and you've taken away the 'art.'

"We've forgotten how to see things for ourselves."

In 1966 at the Los Angeles County Museum of Art Seymour had a show called "I Am Alive." In it were displayed a collection of things he'd found within a 10-mile radius of the museum: a tin can smashed by the tires of a car; the delicate filaments of an electric light bulb; braided challah (egg bread) from a Jewish bakery ("Art is something an artist does; he's got some kind of okay license to be an artist. God forbid the baker could do something creative!"); an antique permanent-wave machine; photographs of ghetto graffiti and storefront churches. He also encouraged people to add to the show, to bring their own discoveries.

"It bothers me that somebody will gaze in awe at an oil painting of a motorcycle, and then ignore the real article," Seymour says.

"Art? Art? I don't know nothing about art," said Mrs. Saavedra, one of "Seymour's people" who built a fantasy world in her front yard — a Christmas decoration that got away from her and became a total environment-assemblage of plaster animals, glittering tinsel, dime-store dolls and winking lights. Seymour had asked her how she went about doing her art, how she'd gotten started.

"Just get rid of your kids," she said emphatically. "That's the only secret. They're always the ones who say, 'Ma, you can't do that. Everybody is going to stare at us.'"

Seymour was born in Chicago in 1935. Seventeen years later the family moved to Los Angeles, where he has lived and worked since, with rare exceptions, within eight blocks of Fairfax Avenue — a thriving neighborhood of Jewish delicatessens, variety stores, bookshops, bakeries and excited street life from Pico to Sunset Boulevard.

When he was thirteen, he was given a camera.

"Well, you see, I had this camera..." Seymour always begins the story of his life.

With it he began to record the "unique, crazy, wonderful" life he saw around him — a revelation after Chicago with its Gothic fastness and constricting winters. Here, everything was freedom, not conformity, experimentation, not tradition. He saw the nervous, shifting, nomadic lifestyle; the exuberant clothes, hairdos, cars, music, dances.

And then Seymour saw the Watts Towers.

In 1952 Marvin Rand, a photographer to whom Seymour was apprenticed for a time, took him out to the Los Angeles ghetto suburb of Watts, on the eastern perimeter of the city. There Simon Rodia, an aged Italian immigrant — a small man, barely five feet tall, who Seymour remembers only as "a tiny fleeting shadow" — had built five fantastic towers of steel and concrete in the yard adjacent to his house. One of the Towers was almost a hundred feet tall.

This work, unbidden and unknown, had occupied Rodia for thirty-three years. He had no money and no one to work with him, though people occasionally brought him things — broken crockery, coke bottles, scraps — to work into his designs.

Critics invariably compare Rodia's towers to Antonio Gaudi's structures. Someone once showed Simon a photograph of Gaudi's immense Sagrada Familia cathedral in Barcelona, a monumental work of narrow towers and bizarre sculpture in the Gothic tradition that is still being built by generations of artisans and stonemasons.

"Did this man have helpers?" Simon asked.

"Yes, he did."

"I had no helpers," Simon replied.

Seymour began photographing the Towers in 1957. He put together a slide show of the Towers using the jazz music of Sonny Rollins to set the mood and pace. In March 1958, however, his documentation of the Towers came to a halt—Seymour got drafted.

Meanwhile, Simon had disappeared. He had left in 1954 and deeded the house and Towers to a neighbor. The property changed hands several times until finally it was sold to Nicholas King and William Cartwright in 1959. When the city declared the Towers a hazard and issued a demolition order that same year, King and Cartwright publicized the danger to the Towers. Their pleas for help attracted architect Ed Farrell, engineer Bud Goldstone and Seymour, who wangled a weekend pass from the army. Together with thirty or forty others, they constituted the "Committee for Simon Rodia's Towers in Watts" which battled the city order. They saw that stress tests were designed and carried out; the Towers stood up to them. They were safe.

After his discharge from the army in 1960, Seymour was eager to resume photographing the Towers. But he felt the only way he could do the job right was to spend months there, night and day, photographing every change of light, every new perspective, every deepening or paling of color in the delicate, coiling web of spires and the walled cloister surrounding them.

So that is precisely what he did. Commissioned by the Los Angeles County Museum in 1961, Seymour spent six months photographing the Towers. Many of the thousands of prints resulting from that epic cycle were exhibited in his show in the L.A. County Museum in 1962. They have since been shown in many major museums and publications dealing with indigenous art and architecture.

But whatever became of Simon Rodia, the sole creator of these wonders? In 1960 Kate Steinitz, archivist for the committee that saved the Towers, found Simon in Martinez, a small town in the Sacramento River delta near San Francisco. A group from the committee went up to meet him and arranged for a slide show of the Towers at the San Francisco Museum of Modern Art.

They asked him if he wanted to go back and live at the Towers again.

"When someone you love has died," he said, "you don't want to talk about them anymore." No one was ever sure that Simon understood that the Towers had been saved. He was eighty-one at that time.

The night of the slide show at the museum, Seymour walked into the building behind Simon, who was dwarfed by the high ceilings, awed by the marble and the gold frames, silent and bewildered. When they walked into the auditorium, two hundred people stood up, cheering and applauding.

"I left Simon then," Seymour says. "He went on in alone. I couldn't do it. I stayed outside.

"I guess it was right about then I realized that somebody like him shouldn't have to wait until he's ninety years old for people to say 'thank you.'"

However, most of the "grand eccentrics," as Seymour calls them, weren't getting any thanks or recognition.

When Seymour first began taking his photographs, it seemed to him that what he was documenting was a fount of human creativity that would never dry up. Many of the "grand eccentrics" were still living; they seemed ageless. But they were not.

Simon died in 1965. John Guidici, whose fabulous backyard labyrinth of cement in Northern California was, until Seymour showed up, an unheralded work of forty-eight years, was nearing ninety when the show, with photographs of his work in it, was hung at the museum. Although he hadn't left his home in many years because of illness, he made a trip to San Francisco with his family to see it. He died two weeks later. Romano Gabriel's fanciful garden of wooden sculpture in Eureka was disintegrating from sun, rain and neglect. Romano was in an old people's home, rarely coherent. Seymour made a trip there to show him an article about his work and to show him the poster from the museum show, which had a picture from Romano's garden. Seymour said he laughed and laughed. He really didn't understand how much people loved his work. Soon after the visit, he died.

"I guess it came as a shock to me that this was a phenomenon that was passing, that these people came along in a certain generation, and there was no one taking their place," Seymour says.

"I began to get frantic when I'd see something great and go back a year later and find a parking lot there, or just nothing. Everyone seems to take it for granted or else they don't care; they think it's junk, has no value because it's not 'art.'"

The pictures in this book represent the exuberant, uninhibited imagination of the people of California. They also represent the life work of Seymour Rosen.

These things Seymour has photographed would have happened without his help, but we would never have known about most of them. His photos depict the essence of California art—the fearlessness of expression, the joy and wonder—at the grassroots level.

Whether the work of others more consciously "artists" evolved from the bizarre and beautiful creations pictured here or whether it was a parallel action isn't important.

Did Los Angeles artists Craig Kauffman and Billy Al Bengston get their slick, shiny "candy-apple" colors from motorcycle painters like Von Dutch Holland, or were they all influenced by the glittering, artificial suns and moons and stars of Hollywood? And who made those?

Which came first, the "Bay Region Art" of sculptors Robert Hudson and William T. Wiley or the junk-assemblage houseboats in Sausalito and the anonymous mudflat constructions of scarecrows and Don Quixotes on the eastern shores of San Francisco Bay? California artist Wayne Thiebaud is fascinated with the way people arrange food on buffet tables, fish in fish-store windows, and he paints that. Which is the "art"? And does it matter?

Whichever came first, the "anonymous" arts or the "fine" ones, California art springs from a teeming chaos of redwood grove mysticism, mountain mysteries, city life, and a funky mix of fetish, ritual, irreverence, Indian lore, pioneer gold rush fantasy, and sunsets. It reflects the many different histories of its people: American Indian, English, Samoan, Mexican, African, German, Filipino, Spanish, Korean, Chinese, Japanese, Swedish.

The combined imagination of the restless souls who live in California is a hotbed of art; a huge and self-perpetuating ecosystem in which some are small, unheralded and ephemeral, others monumental and enduring. All are interdependent, equally vital.

The human achievements pictured in this book are like that area along the coast called the "intertidal zone": a moist, fertile playground of creation close to the deep water, where it all began. It's a submerged world; you have to wade in knee-deep to see the shimmering, spiny, scuttling creatures there—thousands of them, each unique.

Every day, in a world unseen by us (either we take it too much for granted or we simply don't bother to look) are born these strange new forms. What Seymour has done is to give us back something we had lost—the ability to see, hear and feel what our fellow human beings are thinking through the images they create. He shows us that art is not what we are told it is, but what we discover or create; that art is an impulse, an *instinct*, and our birthright; neither masterpiece nor marble, but gestures of the spirit in the void, forming the characters and symbols of the language of life itself.

Beth Coffelt

Watts Towers.

Simon Rodia was a short, lean, uneducated man, who did laborer's work throughout the United States. He settled on a triangular-shaped lot in Watts in 1921 and spent the next thirty-three years building his "Watts Towers." The towers are made of bar metal, which Simon bent by hand, using the nearby railroad tracks as a vise. The metal was over-lapped or butted together, wrapped by hand with wire and enclosed in cement. The cement also held the tiles, seashells, pieces of glass and embossments with which Simon embellished his work. Not a single bolt, weld or rivet holds the towers together.

Simon didn't know he was making engineer-ing breakthroughs, didn't know what hadn't been done or what some people thought couldn't be done — he just needed to do something and get some acknowledgment from people. Everything was accomplished with minimal money, no help and no formal plans.

Costumes.

We all share the need to fantasize. But most adults wait for authorized times to put on costumes and be open with their playfulness. Thank goodness for Halloween, for parades, luaus and street parties. And thank goodness for "Let's Make a Deal." When else would people who have always wanted to dress up as a tuna salad or a cabbage leaf or a firefly get the chance?

Ford Boulevard Elementary School, East Los Angeles 1972

Las Floristas Headdress Ball, Los Angeles 1975

*Left, Jagannatha Cart Festival,
San Francisco 1975*

Las Floristas Headdress Ball, Los Angeles 1975

Let's Make a Deal TV Show, Los Angeles 1975

San Francisco 1975

Japanese New Year's Parade, San Francisco 1972

Freak Ball, Los Angeles 1975

Stations of the Cross Happening, East Los Angeles 1972

Renaissance Fair, Agora 1968

I'm OK.

We all want to do something beautiful, to be somebody, to invent, to participate, to share. And underlying it all is a need to be acknowledged by our peers.

It's a great feeling to dress in a white suit, sit astride a motorbike and marshall the big parade. But sometimes even the joy of a grand performance isn't quite enough. We need the medal, the trophy, the listing in Guinness Book of Records, the tangible evidence that other people have taken notice and appreciate our efforts.

Tournament of Roses, Pasadena 1973

Ferndale Arts Festival, Ferndale 1976

Rose Bowl Swap Meet, Pasadena 1972

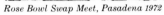

Odd Ball Olympics, Los Angeles 1975

Custom Car Show, Los Angeles 1975

Black Shriners Band Drill and Motorcycle Competition, Los Angeles 1976

DMV. Decorated and Modified Vehicles. In the '50s I was introduced to the custom car and another view of the world by kids who couldn't articulate anything about "art," but lived it by constantly refining their fantasy vehicles. For many in Southern California, custom paint jobs meant Von Dutch Holland. He was the most popular and inventive, an expert at pinstripes, flames and spectacular detailing.

Von Dutch is not an academy artist, but one of the best talks I ever heard on sculpture and form was the one he gave to a guy who came into his garage with a Chevy and wanted a paint job like the one he'd seen on a Von Dutch Ford. "Von" explained that besides not wanting to repeat a design, he couldn't possibly do the same kind of paint job because air flows differently around a Chevy than a Ford.

Von Dutch painted magnificent motorcycle tanks, using thirty or so layers of paint: a primer, a pearl, a couple of clears, a tint and a clear, an image, a couple more layers of clear, another tint, another image. You could look right down into one of those paint jobs. Von's garage was always crowded with doting kids, beer drinkers and a number of future easel artists who adopted his tools, paints, techniques and surfaces and used them in their "fine arts."

In the '60s, hippie kids started painting their vehicles, but not with the skill or delicacy, neatness or finish that the builders of hot rods

Von Dutch Holland, Los Angeles 1960

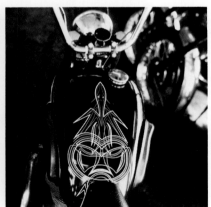

Los Angeles 1972

lavished on theirs. The hippie van, a travelling home, became a symbol of the counterculture. Eventually the van idea was picked up by surfers and then by the vanners who now sport the $1,000 paint job and the $3,000 interior, complete with quadraphonic sound, water beds, carpets and furs, fireplaces, aquariums, skylights, bay windows and bars.

Some of the most lavish cars and motorcycles of all are never driven. They have been converted into pieces of sculpture. Californians by the hundreds of thousands flock to car shows to admire Model T's taken from junk yards and painstakingly restored to perfection, to ooh and ah over etched glass windows, chromed undercarriages, chromed motor and exhaust systems — every inch immaculately clean and neat. (The judges come around with toothpicks and inspect for dirt and oil.) Many show cars are family projects, four or five years in the building. But some car owners, like the Medicis of another era, seek out professional artists — the best chromers, metal benders, upholsterers and painters — to compose their sculpture.

Long Beach 1974

Los Angeles 1972

Anaheim 1975

Long Beach 1972

Long Beach 1975

Anaheim 1975

Los Angeles 1974

Tommy the Greek

Ed "Big Daddy" Roth

Neil Averill

Steve Young

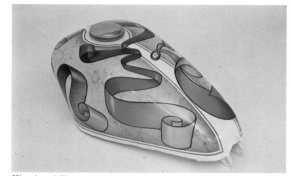

Himsl and Haas

Horst

Audrey Garcia Rawlings

Left, Los Angeles 1966

Dickens 44 Bascom

1972

1975

1971

1972

1972

1972

King City 1975

Old Trapper. After working twenty years as a government trapper in Michigan, John Ehn came to California in 1941, bursting with stories to tell about the old west. He opened a motel, and in 1945 he hired a sculptor to build a huge trapper (modeled after John himself), the first and main character in a western tableau. After watching the sculptor for three days, John decided he'd learned all the necessary technical skills to continue on by himself. He spent the next fifteen years filling the front yard with sculpted characters from history and fiction, and tombstones inscribed with tales of the west. The faces on many of his figures are life masks of his family. "Old Trapper" John moves a little slower than he used to, but he still loves to dress up in his old buckskins and tell how he and the Indians met the last of the cowboys and the last of the badmen.

Shaped Buildings.

After the gold rush, realtors and others created fantastic stories of paradise to attract people to California. Some who came adopted the same flamboyant style to entice each other and the eastern tourist to their individual businesses. The landscape became dotted with three-dimensional tamales and hot dogs, shoe-shaped buildings, concrete tepee motels, drive-through donuts and giant oranges. The phenomenon thrived in the late '30s; its decline is due less to a lack of imagination and whimsy than to building codes and building costs.

East Los Angeles 1971

Bakersfield 1976

Mar Vista 1962

Los Angeles 1968

Los Angeles 1970

La Puente 1975

Near Turlock, Route 99 1976

Rialto 1975

Los Angeles 1971

Los Angeles 1971

Los Angeles 1972

Homemade Ads. Small store owners out of necessity become copywriters, graphic artists and assemblagists. The care and pride of the owner comes through — be it a window display or the way a butcher sculpts the hamburger in the display case. Twenty years after falling in love with hardware store displays, I saw modern artists assembling similar accumulations, framing them and selling them as art. Unfortunately many of the people who were awed in the gallery still don't see the relationship to their daily lives.

South-Central Los Angeles 1969

Los Angeles 1971

Daly City 1971

Los Angeles 1971

Los Angeles 1971

Los Angeles 1972

Herbie Day. Herbie Day at Disneyland. For Disney it was a chance to promote a movie, for the participants a chance to allow their fantasy to soar. Hundreds of Volkswagens—decked out in paint and glitter, crepe paper and ribbon, beans and noodles—vied for prizes. It was a diverse group of people. Some had spent months gathering their materials and ideas. Others just drove up in their everyday cars.

WE'RE HOPING FOR A BEETLE

Anaheim 1974

Desert View Tower.

Desert View Tower was started in 1923 by Robert Vaughn to commemorate the Mormon Trail. In the 1930s M. T. Ratcliffe, an engineer, came to the desolate area to recuperate from tuberculosis and work on the tower. He spent off hours in the surrounding rocks, carving skulls, buffalo, snakes and strange little animals.

Baldessare Forestiere.

The land Baldessare Forestiere bought in the desert turned out to be too hard for farming. Besides, the climate was too hot and there was no wood to build a home. He decided to go underground. In 1906 he began thirty years of working alone with pick and wheelbarrow to carve out a living space. He envisioned Model T's that would drive into an underground courtyard, through a labyrinth of tunnels to a unique subterranean restaurant he would build. Unfortunately, he died before his dream was fulfilled. His family keeps Baldessare's underground haven open, allowing the public to explore his conical-shaped rooms and marvel at the multiple-fruit citrus trees that flourish 15 feet underground beneath hand-carved skylights.

Storefront Churches. There are more than 450 storefront churches in south central Los Angeles alone. Mostly identified by simple handlettered graphics and paintings, they have been personally decorated by parishioners who could not afford real stained glass and had to paint their own. The interiors are generally sparse, but they come alive on Sunday morning.

Watts 1969

Los Angeles 1969

Los Angeles 1971

Los Angeles 1969

Graffiti and Gang Markers.

Throughout history, people have used the walls to let the world know they exist. Cave paintings were the first graffiti. In World War II "Kilroy" was everywhere. Today wealthy benefactors have their names inscribed on bronze plaques; property owners label their buildings; businesses put out signs. City, county and state boundary lines are well identified. Foreign embassies are bits of their own country in another land. All of these are defined by some kind of symbol, and people with no other appropriate means but similar needs make their mark with cans of spray paint.

Middle class neighborhoods go in for interpersonal writings and pronouncements of love. Bathrooms in "sophisticated bars and restaurants" tend towards philosophical statements and puns, while bathrooms in gas and bus stations and the undersides of bridges as well as factory walls carry pornographic drawings without much text. Railroad yards seem to be filled with hobo signs, long poems about life and politics, and statements of passing through.

In some neighborhoods, graffiti are almost a necessary way of life. They are the neighborhood billboard, the key to knowing how feelings are running and what is going on, but you have to know how to read them. The handwriting was literally on the wall in Watts before the streets erupted in riots.

Los Angeles 1962

East Los Angeles 1972

San Francisco 1971

FOUNDING BENEFACTORS

MR AND MRS WESLEY I DUMM
R AND MRS JAMES McALISTER DUQUE
HN AND RELLA FACTOR FOUNDATION
MR AND MRS LOUIS FACTOR
MAX FACTOR MEMORIAL FUND
THE FASHION GROUP INC
FINKELSTEIN FOUNDATION
R AND MRS LEONARD K FIRESTONE
THE FLUOR FOUNDATION
EDWARD T AND JEAN M FOLEY
MR AND MRS THEODORE A FOUCH
MR AND MRS PATRICK J FRAWLEY
MR AND MRS LOUIS J GALEN
AND MRS JOHN JEWETT GARLAND
THE GARRETT CORPORATION
MR AND MRS WILLIAM GOETZ
MR AND MRS SAMUEL GOLDWYN
R AND MRS BENJAMIN GRAHAM

AND MRS COURTLANDT S GROSS
AND MRS ROBERT ELLSWORTH GROSS
ND MRS GORDON GREENE GUIBERSON
R AND MRS PRENTIS COBB HALE
ED AND VIOLA HART FOUNDATION
HARVEY FOUNDATION

KATHARINE BIXBY HOTCHKIS
HUGHES AIRCRAFT COMPANY
THE JAMES IRVINE FOUNDATION
THE ISAACS BROTHERS FOUNDATIO
ELIZABETH BIXBY JANEWAY
MR AND MRS CHARLES DUDLEY JEN
MR AND MRS EARLE M JORGENS
HELEN AND FELIX JUDA FOUNDATI
MR AND MRS WILLARD W KEIT
MRS FREDERICK C KINGSTON
MR AND MRS BURT KLEINER
MR AND MRS TH R KNUDSEN
JOSEPH O AND JULIETTE B KOEPFLI in
SAMUEL H KRESS FOUNDATION
MR AND MRS WILLIAM POWELL LE
MR AND MRS MERVYN LERO
MR AND MRS SOL LESSER
MR AND MRS ERIC LIDOW

FOUNDATION OF THE LITTON IND
THE RALPH B LLOYD FOUNDAT
LOCKHEED AIRCRAFT CORPORAT
MR AND MRS DAVID L LOE
LOS ANGELES HERALD—EXAMIN
MR AND MRS CHARLES LUCK

Los Angeles County Museum of Art 1971

Los Angeles 1974

In Chicano neighborhoods in Los Angeles, the 325 gangs use the walls to stake out and define their territory. Ignoring established political boundaries, they mark their boundaries with their bold graphic symbols, their *placa* or their marker. When individuals sign their names, they identify themselves as belonging to a particular area. Many years before the phrase "in-resident artist" became popular, gangs had their own resident artists, experts with a spray can, who are valued for their inventiveness — and their necessary speed. When a gang wants to expand its territory, a raiding party goes out and writes its *placa* over that of the other gang. The calligraphy of the *placa* has developed in sophistication over the years, and many who have studied it claim they can look at a marker and tell the approximate year and geographic location in which it was done.

Duke Cahill. Duke Cahill is a great accumulator, a collector of post office boxes, water cannons, parts of schoolroom chairs and old-fashioned desks, 15-foot flags, crescent wrenches, iron wheels, old box cars, and countless other things.

From his fiberglassing and plastering business he also accumulated an abundance of empty 55-gallon drums which in 1966 were just cluttering up the yard. It took Duke's inspiration to convert them into a menagerie of martian-like birds, dogs and people.

Duke and his fiberglassing crew spent countless rainy days (when they couldn't do their normal work) stacking the drums and shaping them with plaster, turning metal wheels into gates, and crescent wrenches into a 12-foot filigreed wall covering. They even dribbled cement in the courtyard to create an effect of cobblestones.

In the midst of his fantasy environment Duke now raises llamas, burros and innumerable cats.

Parades. Most parades were once simple community events; today they are an industry run by associations and professionals. An amazing amount of time goes into their preparation and thousands of dollars are spent for costumes. To marching bands and baton twirlers a local parade is a place to compete for that coveted invitation to a major football game or a big international event.

Still, a parade is an opportunity to honor outstanding members of the community, to demonstrate patriotism, to get out in the streets and have fun with family and neighbors. It's also a great place to dress up as an Indian or a cowboy or an Arab prince.

The Tournament of Roses Parade is a yearly ritual that allows thousands of people from the Pasadena/Los Angeles area to participate in an event seen by 150 million people throughout the world. Each year new floats join those resurrected from the "graveyard." Community groups are hired to embellish the floats, petal by petal, flower by flower. A million people sleep in the streets the night before to get good seats for the parade. And for three days after, crowds flock to the post parade area to admire and touch the floats and to have their pictures taken.

Cinco de Mayo, San Francisco 1972

Cinco de Mayo, San Francisco 1972

Korean Parade, Los Angeles 1975

Korean Parade, Los Angeles 1975

Korean Parade, Los Angeles 1975

Fourth of July, Glendale 1975

Tournament of Roses, Pasadena 1973

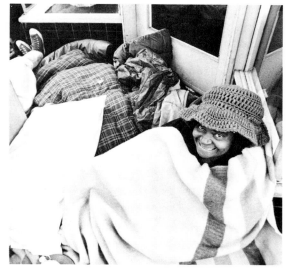

Tournament of Roses, Pasadena 1976

Possum Trot. Not many of the people zooming by on the super highway stopped by Calvin and Ruby Black's rock shop at Possum Trot, so Calvin spent his time carving hundreds of dolls and Ruby dressed them. They put the dolls in tableaux by the side of the road, but still the cars sped by without even slowing down. Then Calvin rigged up windmills on top of the tableaux and attached the dolls; and the wind blew and the dolls moved and the people on the highway stopped. Calvin set up a Fantasy Doll Show. He named the dolls after Lily Langtree and her contemporaries. He covered his body with a black cloth and manipulated the dolls while a tape of his voice in falsetto told stories of the old west.

POSSUM TROT

OPEN

TURQUOISE
INDIAN
MADE
AND JEWELRY
DOLLS

WE DON'T KNOW
WHERE MA IS
BUT WE GOT
POP ON CE

Cola

Albert Glade. Albert Glade came to the United States from Germany in 1907, and built his first garden in Los Angeles in the 1920s. His fourth, the "Enchanted Garden," is a ten-year labor of love, filled with color—bits of plastic and glass, small pictures, shiny things, concrete and ceramic plaques, covered walkways—and enclosed by concrete mud-pie walls. Albert loved to sit in his garden and entertain the neighborhood children with stories of his days in the silent movies.

Albert Glade/89

County Fairs. Some ten million people attend California's county fairs every year. Once a rare chance for rural people to gather and show off the accomplishments of the past year, county fairs are now more and more shared with the urban person in a once-a-year melding of cultures, crafts, arts, husbandry. They represent a continuum of America's heritage and inventiveness.

Los Angeles County Fair, Pomona 1974

Los Angeles County Fair, Pomona 1972

Kern County Fair, Bakersfield 1972

Los Angeles County Fair, Pomona 1972

Kern County Fair, Bakersfield 1974

Los Angeles County Fair, Pomona 1974

Los Angeles County Fair, Pomona 1974

Community Events.

Los Angeles has the second largest Mexican population in the world, yet most of our institutions, including the schools, have not provided much information about the rituals and heritage of the Mexican people. In East Los Angeles a local art group, Self-Help Graphics, decided to fill the void by staging a local "Day of the Dead" festival which involved the whole community.

Slowly more and more communities are developing their own events. Watts has its parades and chalk-ins. In Capitola whole neighborhoods of children and adults work together to build floats and actually float them down the river in the city's wonderful Begonia Festival.

At the Renaissance Faire each summer, thousands of people transport themselves through costume and music, food and entertainment into another place and time.

For us outsiders all these events are chances for insight into other people, chances to participate and to enjoy the real smells and tastes of foods uncompromised for American tastes. For the hosts there is a sense of pride in sharing their heritage.

Cinco de Mayo, Point Richmond 1972

Cinco de Mayo, Point Richmond 1972

Day of the Dead, East Los Angeles 1974

Chalk-In, Watts 1970

Renaissance Fair, Agora 1972

Love-In, Los Angeles 1966

Capitola Begonia Festival 1975

Cherry Blossom Festival, San Francisco 1972

100/Community Events

Kinetic Sculpture Race, Ferndale 1976

Swap Meets. For me a swap meet is an outdoor museum—acres of clothes and tools, toys and junk, but also art nouveau and English furniture, collections of old cigar labels, glassware and photographs, and other things not yet old enough or precious enough to be exhibited in our institutions. But in this museum you can touch and fondle the exhibits, talk to the collector and take home with you whatever catches your fancy.

Rose Bowl Swap Meet, Pasadena 1972

Hulaville.

Miles Mahan did it. He wanted to retire, play golf and write poetry. So he bought 2½ acres and built a three-hole golf course—all sand trap with gopher holes and snake hazards. His poetry is displayed there for all to see.

I hope someday somebody has enough sense to make Miles California's poet laureate and allow him to wander the state painting his poetry on wooden signs and planting them wherever he chooses.

Look north and you will see
A seat up in the Joshua tree
Where a picture you can snap
With a sweetheart in your lap

On one o'leven he sold his wares
In Cathedral City he had no cares
Everybody likes Chuckawalla Slim
And hopes fate will be good to him

Chuckawalla Slim was a mountaineer
Who searched for stones without a fear
In his cottage trailer he had a lapidary
Late hours he worked'n never did tarry

Murals. In the early 1970s, the barrios of San Diego, Los Angeles, San Francisco and Sacramento began turning their walls into political paintings, many imitating the style of the great Mexican muralists and telling stories of the heroes of the Mexican Revolution. Estrada Courts, a housing project in Los Angeles, has more than fifty murals in a two-block area, and another thirty are underway. In San Diego, painters from all over the state are helping paint pylons under the Coronado Bridge as part of a park being built there.

"Fine arts" committees have recently initiated programs like those of local government agencies which for years have supported, encouraged and somewhat formalized the mural movement, doing their best to promote a vital art which is slowly spreading throughout the cities. Since the start of the '70s, independent "non-ethnic" artists, sometimes commissioned by business interests, have also added to the state-wide proliferation of murals.

Matamoros, Los Angeles 1971

Judy Baca and Christina Schlesinger, Venice 1973

Los Angeles Fine Arts Squad 1972

G. Mead, J. Frost and S. Dubiner, San Francisco 1976

Les Grimes, Vernon 1976

Wayne Holwick, Venice 1971

Daniel Martinez, Estrada Courts, East Los Angeles 1975

Frank Romero, East Los Angeles 1972

Estaban Villa, Sacramento 1972

Logan Community Mural, San Diego 1974

Neon. Neon was once dismissed simply as commercial advertising. Old neon is now exhibited in galleries throughout the country, and a generation of artists work specifically in the medium. Sadly, commercial neon is dying out. It is being replaced by cheaper backlit silk screen signs. Enjoy the ones that are left.

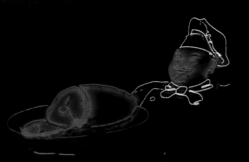

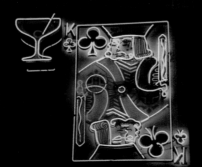

John Guidici. Fifty years ago, John Guidici's son fell into a pond in his backyard and almost drowned. His sister pulled him out. John dumped a bag of cement into the pond, and while it was hardening, he stuck in some seashells and bits of colored glass. So began forty-eight years of building.

Questioned at ninety, John still had no plan for his work. "I just do it," he said. "Sometimes I wake up in the morning and I think of something. Then I go out and I do it. I do this, I do that. At first there was just me and the gophers and the moles. Then people started to bring things. And I find some things. Some people like to go to bars and drink. I like to play with cement."

Pageant of Masters. Every year participants in the Pageant of Masters at Laguna Beach gather to create living replicas of the world's great paintings and sculpture. Local people get to be important historical figures for a while and learn about the works of art through participation. Six million people have seen the Pageant over the last forty-three years.

Germano Charon, Boatmen of Hades 1975

Toulouse-Lautrec, Troupe de Mlle Eglantine 1975

Sanford Darling.

In 1963, at age sixty-eight, Sanford Darling began painting small scenes of places he had visited on two trips around the world. He put the paintings up in his house in Santa Barbara, but very soon he ran out of room. So he nailed his work to the outside of the house and went right on painting—for ten years—on the screens, walls, eaves, doors, refrigerator, chairs, ceilings and rugs. Sanford never tried to sell you a philosophy of life; he just wanted you to return with a couple of kids to enjoy his world.

Tattoo. The tattooer of today is as likely to have an MA degree in art as to be an ex-sailor who just picked up the trade. Today's tattooee, unlike one of "those people" who got tattooed in the past, could be almost anyone. The new tattoo artists view the whole body as a frame rather than seeing the tattoo as an isolated image.

Dean Dennis

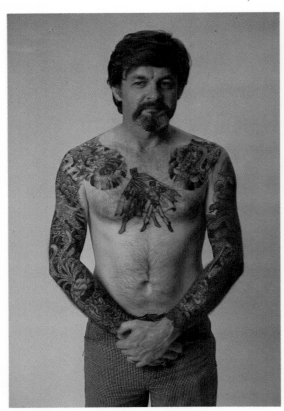

Nightingale and Ed Hardy, Front

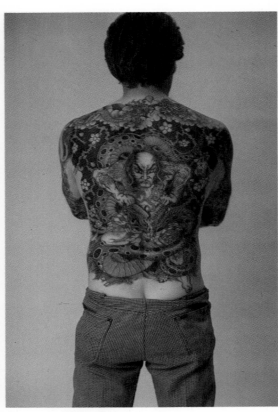

Shore and Ed Hardy, Back

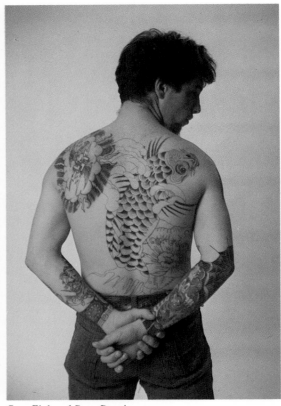

Gary Fink and Dean Dennis

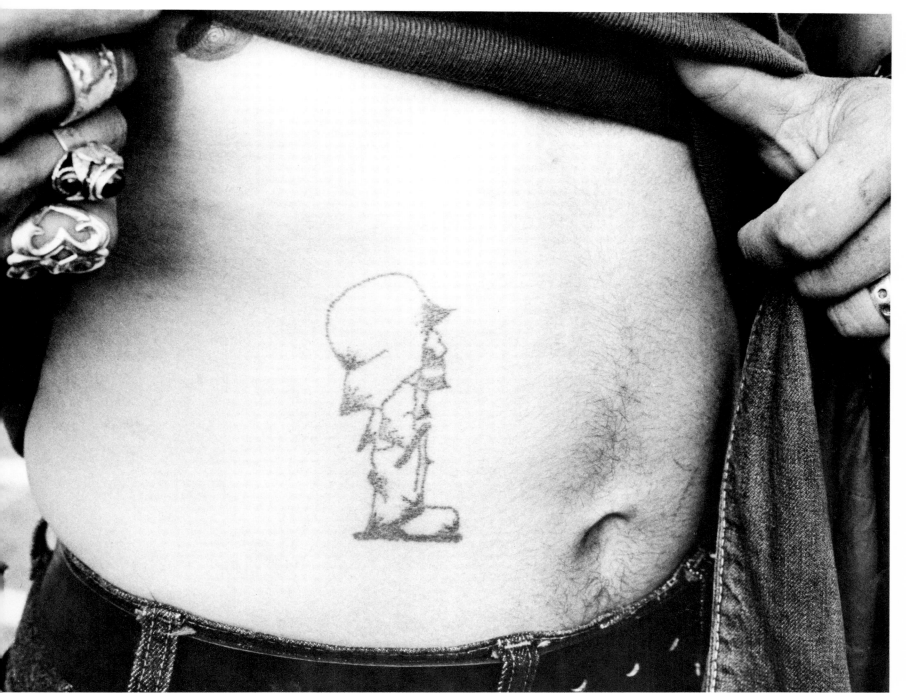

Artist Unknown

Unknown Artist and Lyle Tuttle

Lyle Tuttle

Driftwood Charlie.

In the midst of the desert, William Averett and "Driftwood Charlie" Kasling built their two worlds side by side. Averett, with his one useful arm, built Happy Villa, a series of plaques and maps and tableaux. Kasling created his "world of lost art," a kind of above-ground archeological dig with bas relief and miniature villages. His fantasy animals, sourdoughs with donkeys and amorphous shapes populate an almost formal garden.

When alone, you get the feeling you are the first person ever to stumble on this lost civilization. You are free to fantasize and make up your own history and myths.

Happy Villa by William Averett

Charlie's World of Lost Art by Charles Kasling

138/Driftwood Charlie

Jenner. In the summer, "gypsies" wandering down Highway 1 find the beaches at Jenner loaded with driftwood, which they weave together into houses that are airy and comfortable and as elaborate as energy and inventiveness will allow. In the fall, the ocean sweeps the beach clean—until next year's crop of wanderers comes along.

Emeryville. One of the largest outdoor art exhibits in the country is the spontaneous hodgepodge of anonymous sculpture on the Emeryville mud flats beside the freeway from Berkeley to San Francisco. Whoever is willing to brave the mud can come and produce sculpture from available found material, and add to the exhibit seen by ninety-five thousand people each day.

1971

1978

1973

1978

1973

Romano Gabriel.

Romano Gabriel, a former gardener and carpenter, spent thirty years carving discarded orange crates to create a fantasy forest in his front yard. He populated it with bushes, trees, animals, flowers and caricatures of people, all made of wood. Romano would sometimes hide in part of the garden and, by manipulating ropes and motors, he would make things move—much to the wide-eyed wonder of passersby who didn't know he was there.

Nit Wit Ridge.

Art Beal—he calls himself Dr. Tinkerpaw—is a self-proclaimed "crazy" and stand-up comedian who has spent nearly fifty years building Nit Wit Ridge. Like others, Art used discards and indigenous materials of the area to create his meandering conglomeration of stairs, rooms, patios, fences, grottos, found and stacked objects and continually changing vistas. To make it really come alive, you need Art and his jokes and the warmth shown by his following of young people.

Grandma Prisbrey's Bottle Village.

Tressa Prisbrey, her husband and four children travelled the state working odd jobs until one day in the mid '50s "Grandma" took the wheels off their silver trailer as a hint that she wanted to put down roots. She had accumulated ten thousand pencils in her travels and decided to build a structure to house them. After her pencil house, she just kept on building.

In an old pickup truck, she would drive to the dump where she found her building materials — industrial refuse, personal discards and one of the world's richest veins of old wine bottles. Working alone, Grandma built thirteen houses and nine major and minor structures, all squeezed into a 45- by 275-foot lot.

Her houses are made of bottles and concrete; her walkways are mosaics of pieces of jewelry, scissors, guns, tools, combs, curlers, nails, nuts and bolts. Surrounding it all is a 500-foot bottle-and-concrete fence.

Grandma Prisbrey still bubbles with energy and enthusiasm and wears out much younger people showing them around her bottle village.

Other Environments.

What distinguishes the builders of fantasy environments from most people? I had my theories, but they went very quickly.

What these builders seem to have in common is whimsy, independence and tenacity. Most of them like people, and they like themselves.

They share a sense of caring, especially for small things, and are not awed by "professionals" of any sort. Very few worked from overall plans; their creations just grew.

What seems to make these people different is that they took their dreams and made the time to do something about them.

Fred Von Brant 1975

Herman Fayal 1975

Al Butler 1975

Henry Silverio 1975

Antioch Garau 1962

Otto Roehrick 1975

John Medica 1978

Edward Mathews 1975

Milt Hopkins 1969

Dr. Kenneth Fox 1975

Peter Mason Bond 1972

Bob Zuver 1972.

Tom Sehgrue 1976

George Herzak 1972

Kermit Bishop 1975

C.C. Miller 1972

168/Other Environments

Helen Saavedra 1972

Litto. Emanuel "Litto" Damonte moved to the country to work with his hands and lead a productive and self-sufficient life. He heard no "voices" nor saw any visions of a "masterpiece"; he simply followed his whimsy. He awoke each morning, and if he had an idea or a dream, he would find a way to make it tangible. When he found something wonderful, he added it to his world. It seemed so natural.

I asked him, "Litto, how did everyone let you get away with cluttering up the neighborhood all these years?"

He smiled his proud smile and said, "Look, if I want to go out and get some of that sloppy stuff from the cow and put it into a bucket and throw it on the wall, I'm gonna do it. 'Cause I'm the Boss here."

A Note on the Environments

After a battle with the city of Los Angeles nineteen years ago, the Committee for Simon Rodia's Towers in Watts thought the Towers were saved. But even though they are now internationally known, they are still in jeopardy. And just last year, as we were getting twelve California folk art environments nominated to the National Register, we found that both Romano Gabriel's wood garden in Eureka and the paintings on Sanford Darling's house in Santa Barbara were no longer there.

Al Butler, Albert Glade, John Guidici and Romano Gabriel have recently died. Happy Villa and Charlie's World of Lost Art have been vandalized. Art Beal's Nit Wit Ridge is sliding down the hill. The Underground Gardens in Fresno is only open because of the herculean efforts of Nick and Lorraine Forestiere. Bottle Village and Possum Trot need help—and on and on. These are just the noted ones, and credentialization is only the start.

The problem is not limited to California; it is national in scope. Many wonderful places throughout the country have not yet been noted, and many of the known places have no organized support. These environments "fall between the cracks" of folk art, art and architecture. They fit into no category and, therefore, get no help from endowments or foundations. A few places have been saved, but only through the tenacity of a few caring individuals. There are hundreds throughout the country that will need help.

If you know of any environments or would like to join the effort to preserve this part of America's heritage, please contact me in care of California Living Books, Suite 223, The Hearst Building, Third and Market Streets, San Francisco, California 94103.

Seymour Rosen

Watts Towers. (page 14) Simon Rodia 1879-1965.

Costumes. (page 22) The Let's Make a Deal television show started in 1963. Since then 24,000 have been on the show, with many more showing up to participate.

Old Trapper. (page 42) John Ehn b. 1897.

Desert View Tower. (page 60) Robert Vaughn b. 1878. M.T. Ratcliffe b. 1882. They started in the 1920s. The carvings were begun in the early 1930s, and it was opened to the public in 1950.

Baldessare Forestiere. (page 62) 1879-1946.

Parades. (page 76) Three hundred and seventy parades are held in California each year—adding up to a three-million-dollar business. There have been ninety Tournament of Roses parades.

Possum Trot. (page 83) Calvin Black 1903-1972. Ruby Black b. unknown.

Albert Glade. (page 88) b. 1887 or 1888.

County Fairs. (page 92) There are seventy-seven countywide fairs held in California each year.

Murals. (page 110) There have been approximately 600 murals done in the Los Angeles area since 1970.

John Guidici. (page 118) 1887-1977. Started his garden in 1931 and worked on it for the next forty-five years.

Pageant of Masters. (page 124) There are roughly 850 participants each year in this forty-three-year-old event.

Sanford Darling. (page 126) 1894-1973. Began painting in 1963 and continued until his death.

Driftwood Charlie. (page 135) William Averett started Happy Villa in 1965. Charlie Kasling started his world of lost art in 1968.

Jenner. (page 141) Building on the beach at Jenner began in the late sixties.

Emeryville. (page 143) People started creating sculptures on the mud flats in 1953.

Romano Gabriel. (page 145) b. 1890s d. 1977.

Nit Wit Ridge. (page 152) Art Beal (Dr. Tinkerpaw) b. 1896. Began building in 1928.

Grandma Prisbrey's. (page 156) Tressa Prisbrey b. 1896. Started building in the 1950s.

Other Environments. (page 162) Henry Silverio b. 1894, Otto Roehrick b. 1925. Kermit Bishop b. 1909.

Litto. (page 170) Emanuel "Litto" Damonte b. 1892.